TESTAMENTS OF THE SOUL

Lasheka Lee

authorHOUSE

AuthorHouse™
1663 Liberty Drive
Bloomington, IN 47403
www.authorhouse.com
Phone: 833-262-8899

© 2024 Lasheka Lee. All rights reserved.

No part of this book may be reproduced, stored in a retrieval system, or transmitted by any means without the written permission of the author.

Published by AuthorHouse 11/05/2024

ISBN: 979-8-8230-3564-4 (sc)
ISBN: 979-8-8230-3563-7 (e)

Library of Congress Control Number: 2024921850

Print information available on the last page.

Any people depicted in stock imagery provided by Getty Images are models, and such images are being used for illustrative purposes only.
Certain stock imagery © Getty Images.

This book is printed on acid-free paper.

Because of the dynamic nature of the Internet, any web addresses or links contained in this book may have changed since publication and may no longer be valid. The views expressed in this work are solely those of the author and do not necessarily reflect the views of the publisher, and the publisher hereby disclaims any responsibility for them.

Dear Mom, aka Mary Lee……..

Thank you for giving me the idea to write a Poetry book. You always loved my poems and appreciated the poems I wrote about you. Mom, I wish you were still here today. You have been my angel for so many years since you passed away and I thank you for that blessing of being here in spirit always. It may not be the same but I still continue to appreciate all that you do. I feel your presence especially when I see 11:11 every day, I just know that it is you. Your birthdate 11/11/51 I still hear you saying it so clearly over the phone and when I see 11:11 each day I hear you and it gives me the strength to continue to move forward with what the Lord has for me to do.

Love you Mom,

Your Loving Daughter, Lasheka Lee

Contents

Introduction ix
Acknowledgments xi

Lifeless 1
Friendly Inspirations!.. 2
Since You Been Gone 3
Happy 4
Radio 5
Thanksgiving 6
Christmas 7
Mirror 8
Happy Birthday Brother... 9
Forgetting 10
By My Side 11
Your Smile 12
The Greatest Poem 13
Happy Brithday Sister 14
I Want To Be 15
A Long Year 16
Mom 17
Entertaining An Angel 19
Nobody Understands 20
Pieces 21
Eyes Wide Open 22
Just For One Second! 23
Things Happen 24
Happy Birthday 25
The Greatest Comforter 26
Comfort 27
Our Friendship 28
Just Awesome 29
I Am Ready For Love 30

My Loud Soul	31
It's Raining	32
For This I Thank You	33
Dear Love	34
Words	35
No Better Love	36
Happy Fathers' Day	37
To My God	38
Do I Exist	39
Graduation	40
Happy Birthday Sister-In-Law	41
The Best Mom	42
My First Valentine	43
Father Forgive Me	44
The Question Unknown	45
Chosen By God	46
They Say	47
The Wall	48
Is It Real	49
Waited	50
Help Me Lord	51
Strong	52
Soul Reflections	55
The Lord Is My Poetry	56
Conversations	57
Equally Yoked Souls	58
Unknown Prayer Sauce	59
When a Mother Prays & Love	60
A Blessing from The Lord	61
Family	62

Introduction

For many years, I have been writing poems and through the advice of family & friends I decided that it was time to put together a book highlighting some of the many poems that I have wrote. <u>Testaments of the Soul</u> is my first book & I hope it will be a success! A lot of the Inspiration behind my poems came from my mom Mary Ann Lee who passed away in 2011. I feel my life is just beginning & there will be many more testaments in store.

Now that some time has passed, 12 years to be exact I am happy to be re-launching my book Testaments of the Soul. I know this will be a success!!

I have learned a lot and put my soul in this re-launch. Included are 8 bonus poems to enjoy!

Acknowledgments

I would like to acknowledge my awesome family: Vernon Lee (dad), Talonda Johnson, (sister), Vernon Lachell Lee (brother), Monique Lee(sister) Damian Johnson, Keshaun Johnson, Kylan Lee, Ashton Lee(nephews) Syreeta Lee (sister-in-law) & Alora, Amilya Johnson (great nieces). I would like to thank them for being such a wonderful family & always believing in me. I would also like to thank my partner, Candice Fleming & my best friend Quen Ward for their support.

A big thanks to Romona Jackson (Coach) for your advice.

I would like to thank the rest of my family and friends for their love & support.

I would also like to give thanks to my Lord & savior Jesus Christ because none of this would have been possible without him. Thank you my Lord.

***WELCOME TO THE RE-LAUNCH OF
TESTAMENTS OF THE SOUL***

*May you be blessed and may
these poems bless your soul*

Testaments of the Soul is a book of poems based on my life and others who have shared their life experiences with me. The different poems depicts many feelings & emotions that is a part of life. There are also seasonal poems, birthday poems and many more different types of poem that helps make up this book. Inspired by many Testaments of the soul is written purely from the heart and it captures the different pieces of us all that makes up our soul.

Lifeless

I feel like I'm in a dream & that the soul that's suppose to be in my body is no longer here. I walk through life feeling helpless inside & like a liar because when people ask I tell them that I'm doing just fine. When I stand up to walk I'm always trembling inside because I have but a little energy to walk & it's becoming hard to hide. No one cares to listen or to see the pain in my eyes but it's not their fault because I'm always in disguise. I sit alone thinking why do I even have life because being alone while surrounded by the world is an empty feeling that I don't like. If you could really see how I'm feeling it would be one of the saddest things you ever seen & you would probably wonder how in the hell I can get up each morning & live. A lot of the feelings that I have I can't even describe but they are not good but awful feelings that I try my best to hide. Why is my life like this I don't really know but I just feel like nothing & that I'm just here for show.

Friendly Inspirations!

It just wouldn't feel right if I didn't write this.
Especially since I was inspired I just couldn't resist.
From early ages we formed a bond that was truly heaven sent
& a friendship vibe that was our own that we only get.
Why did we become friends?
It was the will of god to enhance & brighten our life
while substaining an awesome bond,
that throughout life has been tested several times.
Right or wrong we learned our lessons each & everytime.
Never giving up or forgetting our friendship
being a blessing that has subststained the test of time.
You are truly special & unique in everyway,
one of the best blessings I ever received in my life
& I thank God for blessing me & showering me
with his favor in that way.
Due to my foolishness I lost the trust you had given to me
& I know this might sound crazy
but that was the best thing that could have happened to me.
You see I wouldn't know how much
I was blessed up until that day.
I can't imagine never knowing you
& I feel very blessed to miss you today.

Since You Been Gone

It's been several months momma since you passed away and it still hurt just as much as if it was still that day. I wash in my tears a couple days out the week and when it looks as if i'm fine it's because I am numb from weeping that week. I hide behind my glasses so the hurt doesn't show and my smile some days when it's strong enough to hold. I take it one day at a time knowing that's what you would want but it hurt so bad momma and this ain't no joke. I focus on the positive keeping the negative away but when I focus on your smile I get washed away, in the tears that I cry now which are tears of joy. Realizing you live in me makes me strong. Strong enough to withstand anything that comes my way, being easy to forgive and trusting in the lord always. You left me alot of knowledge that I will always keep. I can only hope I can be half the woman you were so I can smile and laugh everyday of the week. I love you momma!!

Happy

Nothing can even begin to describe the joy & happiness I feel inside. Each day I live it to the fullest not wasting my time. Positive thinking is what I do negativity has no place. Giving, encouraging and helping others are in my soul for whoever is in need of any of those things. My heart is always open to anyone who has lost anyone or anything. Just remember through lost soon will come gain which will equal less pain or no pain. The joy & happiness that I'm feeling didn't come from anyone or anything. It comes from something greater that neither you nor I can explain. I'm not perfect and I never claimed to be but I'm not letting that or no one stop me from being the best that I can be. I feel so good now that I wish I can give this feeling to others too. If you focus on all the good things in your life then you will start feeling good too!

Radio

As you turn the radio dial to the sounds of my life you will hear my heart playing victory & joy with a mixture of nice. Not too long ago my station was different, it played hurt & pain mixed with emptiness. Now that my heart is playing victory alot of things have changed. My life is picking up now and I am so happy for the change. No more interference from other stations that time has passed. My life is clearer now and my heart is on blast. No way am I going to change the station now, it sounds too good! So I am going to make it last and turn it up some more to share the tunes!

Thanksgiving

Let me give thanks to the creator of my life not just for thanksgiving but for every day of my life. To all my friends and family I love you very much. Just hearing from and seeing you all another day is thanks enough. This thanksgiving is very special to my heart. It's the first one without my mom who is very dear to my heart. So mom I'm dedicating this thanksgiving to you. I'm putting my heart in it to enhance the flavor of the food. A heart filled up with love for you that was more than enough and will live on through the food. So mom cheers this thanksgiving is for you. I love you very much momma and I give thanks to you!

Christmas

What do you want for Christmas was the question I was asked. What I want I already have and none of it can be gift-wrapped. See I'm a giver and I like to brighten up people days. My gift is being able to give among many other things. Not just on Christmas but any day that I choose. I'm very blessed to be able to do all the things that I do. So what I want for Christmas is nothing at all because I have all I need and no gift under any Christmas tree can compare with it at all!

Mirror

Look into the mirror and tell me who you see. Is it the person you are inside or the person others want you to be. Do you put on a show and act all fake or do you show the truth, the person you are inside every day. Your reflections in the mirror should always be true. Only you and God will actually know the truth. So if your reflection in the mirror is not really you then keep looking in the mirror until you see the truth!

Happy Birthday Brother

Happy birthday brother dear! You mean so much to me. You are the epitome of what every brother & man should be. I am so very proud of you and the man you have grown up to be. I am so happy that you are my brother and I thank you for all that you have & continue to do for me. A blessing is what you are to me & if there was a better word to describe you then that's what you would be to me. So happy birthday brother and many more to come. I thank God for blessing me with a wonderful brother like you, I couldn't imagine a better one!

Forgetting

Why people always seem to forget all that you've done for them & the minute you make a mistake that's all that you are to them. You do a hundred things right then make one wrong move that to them paint a portrait of your life & now to them that's how you are understood. Through good & bad you have been there to the end & forgiving always when it comes to them. This is the question that comes to my mind, to be quite honest it's hard to define, why someone would want to treat you that way. It is as if they can cast the first stone because they are perfect always. The best answer that I can come up with to this, is if you are treated this way by anyone be the bigger person & maybe it will rub off on them!

By My Side

I'm surrounded by your love every single day. You never leave my side you guide me through every day. Even when I stumble you are there to pick me up. Your love shines through me and every single morning it's always there to wake me up. You protect me every day and you are always there when I need you. An awesome comforter indeed and everything when I need you. A love like yours is truly one of a kind, so I'm going to praise you Lord and love you infinity times the end of time!!

Your Smile

It's in your smile how much you care for me
you never frown when you are in my proximity.
Your smile shines straight through to my heart
where it warms it & keeps it pumping faster nonstop.
You have open me up to something special
that I've never known. A world filled with much
more happiness then I've ever known. When you
look at me it's like your eyes are writing a song
that only plays when our eyes connect in a
frequency that's our own. I didn't know that a
smile could ever make me feel this way, that's
why when we first met you really didn't have
to speak because your smile said everything.
It's the warmest greeting I've ever gotten
& the tightest line that I ever heard. A smile
from you to me has completely changed my
world. You smiled your way into my life & now
we are smiling together. I can't believe you
got me with your smile & captured my heart
forever.

The Greatest Poem

The greatest poem by me is the one that haven't been written. If you understand, what I mean then you understand how I'm feeling. Through the straight & narrow roads & the roads that's never ending. It teaches you about life & helps you grow from experiences. There may be times that you are hurting but no one understands how you are feeling. Just put your trust in the lord & he will heal those broken feelings. True happiness is in your heart & through there love should be giving to everyone who has breath, including yourself. Forgiveness is a priority it's not up for debate. Just ask the Lord & you will see when it's all said & done who will be going through those pearly gates. If you can help somebody then help them & if you can do for them then do. If you have been blessed to do those things then do whatever you can do. Time is flying by & so many people are passing too. If you are not living a fulfilled life yet then ask the lord to direct your steps. So, you can get taken over by his favor & be able to be a blessing to someone else. Then soon you will begin to see all the Lord has for you & all that you ever hoped for want compare to the fulfilled life he has for you.

Happy Brithday Sister

Happy birthday sister!! God is good & god is great!
Thank you god for giving me a fantastic sister
who I love to day, tomorrow & always.
You are a super woman & I look up to you everyday.
I never seen anyone as determined as you seek out
& get all that you've set out to get &
this is not just one time it's always.
When god bless me with children
I hope to be an awesome mother like you
& be able to raise such awesome kids not one but two!
You are always there for me especially when I need some advice.
Without a doubt you always know what to say to make things right.
So sister my dear I hope this to be true,
I hope that everyone could have a sister like you in their life
or at least someone like you! I hope everyday is a happy
occasion for you, especially today because this is the
day God blessed us all with you & if I could change anything
about you I wouldn't change a thing!!
Happy birthday!!!!!

I Want To Be

I want to be rich & drenched with all the treasures that rains down from heaven & be surrounded by everything God wants in my life now until forever. I want to be rich with favour only God can provide, so much favour that it overtakes me & posses me inside. I want to be rich with love, dedication, wisdom & peace & walk with God not with standing going after his heart everyday of the week. I want to be rich with thanksgiving all the time & make God smile just by knowing that I'm his child. These are all the things God has blessed me with all because I'm his child & I asked so he blessed me with all these wonderful gifts!

A Long Year

It's been a year momma since you went home to be with the lord & everyday I miss you & wonder why you are gone. I find myself somedays calling your name or about to call you on the phone but then I remember that you are now at home with the Lord. I never thought about you ever being gone at all. I just thought that everyday I would see you because you're my mom. You are one of the best things that's ever happen in my life & I thank you for giving me such a beautiful life. You were the sweetest, kindness person that I ever known & you were always on fire singing praises to the lord. Momma you taught me so much & did so much for me. I am going to continue doing one of the main things you taught me & that's treating others how I would want them to treat me. I still love you the same as if you were still here. The Lord really showed his favour when he blessed me with you as my mom for all those years. I will forever thank & praise the Lord for giving me such a wonderful gift & mom you will forever be loved & missed!!! I love you mommy.

Mom

Please tell me that I am dreaming because this
just can't be true
my mother has passed away and now
my heart is blue. The happiness
in my life is now gone away and the excitement I
once felt has passed
away too. Please wake me from this
terrible coma nightmare because
it's not funny and that's the truth. Please
pinch me and tell me this isn't true. I miss your
laugh your smile and everything about
you. Reality hasn't kicked in because
I am telling you this just can't be true, how
could a loving person who loved
the Lord be gone so quickly I don't understand
do you. I love you with all my heart
and now its halfway empty and blue. The
blood that once pumped through
it to keep it going has now halfway
passed away with you. It seems like
yesterday you was here with me telling

me what to do and now the

sunshine in my life has been eclipsed

and there is no more sunlight

in my life shining from you. I know I have to move

on because that's

what you would want me to do.

Please momma shine down on me

now as I continue to try to move on

without you. I love you momma!

Entertaining An Angel

They say we entertain angels without knowing it, I found this to be true.
You see I entertain an angel for 29 years and now that angel is gone
and has passed on a powerful love that I will endure.
That angel was such a blessing in my life and
even though that angel is gone,
that powerful blessing is still with me today.
How did I get favored by the Lord to be born of an angel
but not know it until today.
I often wondered how a mother could be so kind, generous,
caring, loving, thoughtful and always the same every day.
What I didn't know is that she was an angel
that the Lord had in my life all those many days.
Thank you Lord for such a wonderful angel
whose love I will share with others today and always.
To have had that angel in my life for such a long time
lets me know that I am highly favored and will praise you always!

Nobody Understands

Nobody understands how I feel on the inside, everyday I cry alone and not just on the inside. Each passing day makes me think, think about what I'm really doing here but then my heart sank, into a pit of curiosity and then suddenly I am all over the place. That answer haven't came yet and I don't know why. Time doesn't stop for no one it just keep going by and I just want to know the answer to this question before time pass me by. I am here right now but this wasted time is making me sick! Nobody understands this feeling I have on the inside, a feeling of emptiness and loneliness that nobody can fix! I cry alone not just on the inside so I want be so sick, sick of a void in my life that I or nobody could seem to fix. What am I doing here? I need the answer now before time pass me by, time that seem as if it's being wasted for what? I don't understand I need an answer now!

Pieces

My feelings are like pieces of a puzzle all mixed up,
I put them in the wrong places and they don't matchup.
I am suppose to be a masterpiece and clearly defined
but my definition is confusion and it's hard to hide.
With all these pieces all out of place,
anyone can clearly see they are misplaced.
Feeling that the pieces are right when you know
they are so wrong,
makes me wonder why I have these pieces at all.
I am trying to put this masterpiece back
together again
and put those pieces out of place in the place
they should had always been.
So, hopefully pretty soon a
masterpiece will emerge
and nothing will come along and mix up my
pieces again,
and my masterpiece will remain
unharmed and undisturbed.

Eyes Wide Open

I'm surrounded by the world

but feel so all alone.

With no one to talk to I feel like a lonely soul.

I'm speaking really loud but

no one cares to listen.

I cover my feelings with a smile and

My feelings get so twisted.

I'm always there to lend a hand, with my ear wide

open, to whoever's in need

and whoever heart may have gotten broken.

I wear my heart on my sleeve and

it feels like its choking.

Choking from loneliness and

splitting from the unspoken.

The world eyes is wide open but they don't see me,

even the ones

that I know look right through me, as if they

don't care, they act

like they don't even know me, like I'm

a stranger in their site but still

their eyes are wide open.

Just For One Second!

Just for one second my world went blank.
The numbness inside me nearly made me faint.
I felt a feeling I never felt before. It's a
feeling I never want to feel again forever more. This feeling
made me want throw up, I can't
even began to tell you how I felt inside because
I was all torn up. This was the longest painful second
that I ever endured in my life. I thought time moved
fast but this was a second that seemed to last a lifetime.
Everything was moving in slow motion and I
could barely catch my breath. I think my heart
may had stopped for half a second before I took
another breath. When I heard you was ok my life went
back into motion. Just for one second my life could have changed
and remained motionless. I am so glad God smiled on you
that day. Now I can breathe much better knowing
that second is over and you are here with me today!

Things Happen

Why do things happen to good people? That is something that we will never know. Through trials & tribulations only god can answer the questions to answers unknown. Just trust in him & then you will began to understand that the plan he has in mind is clearly over all our heads. Even though it don't seem fair just trust in God, so you can have a testimony that you can share with them all. If anybody can fix it you know He can & He always knows what's best because that's His plan.

Happy Birthday

This is a very special day for you, one
that I hope you will enjoy.

You see God rained down his blessings
on this day the day you were born.

Days go by, weeks too.

When this day comes back around it shows
how good God has been to this world and you
too. So celebrate this day and be joyful too!

Because it's not just a blessing for you
it's a blessing to everyone in this
world that knows you!

Happy birthday!!!!!!

The Greatest Comforter

There isn't nobody on this earth that can
understand how you feel
or can speak the pain away to dry up each tear.
The pain alone can numb your soul and make
you question the things that's unknown.
I know the best comforter of them all.
One who has the power to make your soul
smile and stand tall.
Who through good and bad if you just listen,
he breath the answers through your soul
and fill the void that's missing.
So take whole of the greatest power of them all
and he will help you endure through it all.
If at anytime you feel your soul slipping,
you feeling really lonely inside
and your heart is dipping where you
don't want it to go and you trying
hard to be very strong. Just remember
one thing that's written in the word.
That no weapon formed against you shall prosper.
This is the way, the truth, the life and the word!

Comfort

*There is nobody on this earth that knows
what you are going through,
it's because every situation is different
so nobody can even begin to know
how you are feeling but you.
The loss of a mother is truly sad indeed.
There is nobody that would ever or could ever
take the place of such a blessing of a
mother you had no one indeed.
Hold on to the good memories
and never let them go.
Find what works for you and grieve however you
feel so.
Comfort is what you need and
comfort is what you will get.
Just ask the Lord for it and he will comfort you
and comfort from the Lord is as good as it gets.
There is no one on this earth that can
comfort you like the Lord can.
So try Him and He will fix it for you.
Believe me I know from experience that He can.*

Our Friendship

We met a long time ago
unexpectantly in class, you
talked to me and I talked to you
and now time has passed.
But somewhere down the path
our friendship took a plunder, and we
got thrown off the path as if
we tripped and stumbled.
I didn't hear from you no more and
you didn't hear from me either.
But through the grace of God we found
each other again oh what a blessing!
To think I had just found you again only
to mess up this blessing, hurt me
deep inside and through all of
this I learned a lesson!
Your friendship is very special to me like all
Friendships are!
But through the grace of God we
found each other again and just
think I almost ruined it all!
I want us to be good friends the best friends
that we could be. I am not going
to mess up again this
blessing that God has bestowed upon me!!

Just Awesome

My Lord my heart is pouring out with praises
for you. You are so incredible, wonderful
& always there for me too. I am truly happy that
you are guiding my life & blessing me to be
a blessing to others both day & night. Encouraging
others is something I like to do because it brings
me great joy to show them how to get the victory
that I have & that you have for them too. I
thank you for blessing me in every area of my
life & loving me passed my faults & still blessing
me in spite. My Lord I just love me some you &
I will forever sing praises out my heart for you.

I Am Ready For Love

I don't think people understand what I am going through.
I am burning up inside I don't know what to do.
The days are going by the weeks are going by too.
By the time I blink my eye another year has gone by.
I am so ready to find true love I don't know what to do. Longing
for it and being impatient is what I tend to do. Oh somebody tell
me is love really true. I am not
getting any younger and neither are you. Hey aren't you
ready to find me like I am ready to find you. Here I am, come and get
me because I'm so ready for you.

My Loud Soul

My soul is crying out loud but nobody hears it.

I'm so miserable inside but no one can see it.

I walk around in disguise with a big smile on

my face even though I am miserable but I don't show

no trace. When will it be my time to shine

because being lonely inside is getting to be very

typical of my everyday life which when I wear

my disguise is so hypocritical. What am I to do when

I do so much for others and get nothing in return

which is so typical. Should I stop wearing my smile

so I want be hypocritical. Only time will tell and until

then maybe I shouldn't be so critical of everything and

just hope for a miracle.

It's Raining

Each drop represents a mistake I have made. I am trying to
swim but I am drowning from the drops I made. Lakes are
everywhere and little land is in sight.
Lifeguards are miles away and I am nowhere in their site.
This rain keeps on falling and I need to get up onto a boat
because these waves are getting rough. I am
no surfer and I never claim to be but I need someone
to come rescue me. Now I am looking around and I'm so
far away. Water is coming from
all directions and all I can see is rain. I want it
to stop, I want it to go away. Somebody please save
me. I am so ready for the rain to stop and for the sun to come
out and stay.

For This I Thank You

Creativity is a gift you blessed me with and for that
I thank you. Being born of a mother who loved you and put
you first again I thank you. For righting all my wrongs and
restoring my life to be better than it's ever been
I thank you. For experiencing all the things I have and
learning from my mistakes even though they may
have hurt sometimes I thank you. For your love you
shine on me each and every day I thank you. For taking time
out to listen to me talk I thank you. For seeing nothing but
the best in me and good that I do I thank you. Most
of all I thank you for sacrificing your son for me so that I
may live this wonderful blessed life, and your forgiveness
of all my sins. Lord almighty I thank you.

Dear Love

Your compassion touches my soul and releases a happiness that I never known. Your smile is wonderful and keeps me warm. Sometimes I get scared and tremble inside. Your words are so beautiful and make me feel special on the inside. Each stroke of your words makes my heart skip a beat. My whole body feels the heat. Now my body is warming up inside creating an outer glow, one that shines so bright I have to stand outdoors. So dear love I am glad I found you and I never want to let you go. Your love is wonderful and it's more then I could have ever asked for.

Words

They say watch what you say or the words you use because you are bringing things into existence that may not be good for you. The lord spoke this world into existence that's the power of words. So to use them incorrectly could destroy the world. So anything you say or any word you use should be as positive as can be for the sake of you. For if you ask it should be given unto you. So I will continue to use positive words asking and believing for the best because if the lord spoke this world into existence just imagine what you can do.

No Better Love

What God has brought together let no one tear apart. Only a few
will know how it feels to truly be in
love with the right person and you two are among the
few. Haters may come along but they don't have
nothing on you two. Marriage has its aches and pains but with
God the pain don't last always. You may ask the lord
why sometimes and never know the answer. Just
know that our God is a just god and no matter what you may
be going though, it can't compare to the love he has for
you. Our God is good and he is getting ready to bless you
two. You may not see it now but I do and hopefully soon
you will too.

Happy Fathers' Day

First of all let me say forgive me daddy for not saying these words as often as I should. The words are I love you and appreciate you for always doing all that you could. Providing for and protecting our family as a whole shows why God made you head of the household. Today I honor and acknowledge the great father that you are and thank god for blessing me with the greatest father of them all. Happy Fathers' day.

To My God

I have never loved anyone as much as I love you. Every morning your love for me wakes me up and makes me feel brand new. When you speak to me I feel your power all the way through and the love in your voice overwhelms my heart for all the love I have for you. Thank you for blessing me with all things I want as long as I believe and honor you. I have never had anyone promise the things that you have promised and they come true. The sacrifice you made for me shows me how much you love and care for me too. I know I can never love you enough to compare to how much you love me. I love you very much and I thank you for blessing me with your unconditional love always for me.

Do I Exist

Surrounded by silence with no way out.

The only time there is sound is when you scream and shout.

With feelings of loneliness and self doubt

coming out as tears with every single drop.

Is it a way out when no one is around.

Is it possible anyone can hear you if you make a sound.

These are the questions that I ask about life.

It's like you're surrounded by deaf people that has lost their sight.

Are you really there or have you lost your mind.

With feelings of craziness flowing through your mind and thoughts

of insanity being clearly defined to everyone except you.

Graduation

To graduate from anything is a wonderful success!

All your hard work has paid off

and now you can take a little break and rest!

This is just the beginning but you have already passed the test!

The test to take an even bigger step in life

knowing more now and being at your best.

So congratulations to you on this wonderful day!

This is a big accomplishment so be proud

and always remember this special day!

Happy Birthday Sister-In-Law

I glanced at the sister-in-law cards and walked right by. That is not what you are to me you are my sister now. I am happy that my brother was blessed to meet someone like you. That lets me know God is awesome and soon I will be blessed in that way too. Happy birthday sister and many more to come. I hope you have a blessed birthday because you deserve that and so much more.

The Best Mom

What a wonderful gift it is to be able to call you my mother. God out done himself when he blessed the world with you. To know that I came from a woman as smart and great as you, lets me know that I have the favor of God on me just like you. My heart is full of love for you and just by seeing all the things you do for me lets me know you love me too. There is no treasure on earth that could compare to all the tender love and care you have given me all these years. I wouldn't trade it in at all not even if the world asked me.

My First Valentine

I've wanted a valentine for as long as I can remember. Wondering
what year he would come was not so simple. Watching other
couples celebrate this day made me fantasize about
how truly wonderful it is to have a sweetheart for valentines'.
Imagining if my hands will tremble when he pull out a bouquet
of roses and a lovely gift. Wouldn't it be beautiful if he chose
this day to propose so it will symbolize all the
love we have drowning us both. Wow this could be so
special for me and so unique. I can't wait to see the day when I
have my first and last valentines' who will be my husband to be.

Father Forgive Me

Forgive me father for I have sinned. The way of life that I have been living will surely be my end. If I don't straighten up and represent you right, I feel in my heart that I want see the light. The light that you shine down on us from heaven from up above, I feel if I go to those pearly gates I want hear you say servant job well done. To think of the sacrifice you made for us and not show appreciation for all you have done makes me feel ashamed for my many sins and makes me want to correct all the wrong I ever done. So I am keeping it real oh father please hear me now, as I have confess all my sins to you and ask you to forgive me right now.

The Question Unknown

What I want to do with my life is a question unknown. What I am doing right now isn't helping at all. Striving for excellence is what I am about but not knowing what to do with my life makes me want to twist and shout. Thinking positive and not negative is what I've learned. Putting God first in every area of my life is what I need to do so I have heard. Focusing on the good and not the bad is one of my goals. Which path do I take to answer the question unknown.

Chosen By God

I knew one day I would fall in love thank God it's with you.
It was well worth the wait to end up with a blessing of a man like you.
You are the definition of love and now my heart beats for you.
I know God pours out his favor on people but he drowned
me with his favor the day he introduced me to you. You
brought so much joy in my life that I never could imagined and every
day I have to pinch myself to see if this is all true.
They use to tell me to be careful what
I ask for well I thank God I ended up with you.

They Say

I want to be happy just about everyone do. They say happiness comes from the inside but is that really true. If nothing is going right and things around you are falling down should I be smiling and happy keeping my frown upside down. Some say you shouldn't let your circumstances shape how you feel.

Tell me how could they tell you that if they haven't been through the same ordeal. Yea I know they say have faith but I'm a human and I am not perfect neither are you. How could someone tell you how to be happy and where it should come from if they are not you.

The Wall

I am staring at the wall staring into my life. Taking out the wrong
thoughts replacing them with the right. With all
kinds of memories floating around in my head
I stare at the wall to clear my head. I stared long enough
& developed a better way of thinking. I began seeing
clearer painting the wall with my clear thoughts & pure feelings.
The development of being more patient while staring at
the wall is a wonderful thing & the peace it brings makes you
want to stare at the wall all day. Staring at the wall is a very
helpful & powerful tool. If used correctly you can paint a whole
living room, dining room & bedroom.

Is It Real

I use to think it wasn't real. I use to think

that it wasn't true, like hitting the

lottery could it really happen to you. Now

I know it's real, now I know its true.

I feel like the richest person in the world now that I've found you.

When you take me in your arms it feels real good. I have to

pinch myself to make sure this is all true. Your love takes me real high

to a place I never been and it keeps getting higher, I don't know

how to feel. You see this is real new and I've never felt it before and

I want to keep feeling it more and more. Now I know love

is real, now I know love is true. They say fairytales doesn't

happen but it happened to me and you.

Waited

The Lord has rained down his blessings on me, you are the love that I waited for so patiently. Our hearts are connected and full of love so endlessly. This is the love I waited for and it feels so good to me. No one but God compares to the love you have for me. I feel your love when you are looking at me. If a kiss could tell it all your kiss would tell how good you are to me and how very deeply you are in love with me. My passion is the same as your passion is for me. Love is good and I'm so glad it happened to me.

Help Me Lord

Help me Lord I don't know what to do. My life is in shambles and I feel so blue. Nobody seems to care no one but you.
Please lord hear me now and fill my life with you. I need freshness in my life and people who care and treat me right. The way things are going I'm about to go crazy I swear. I do to much good to be treated so badly. To be disrespected seems like always and unhappy and sad. This is not fair. Lord tell me why are these things happening to me. I need you lord right now please Lord listen to me. My heart is full of sorrow and my soul is to. I've searched everywhere for help oh lord I need you. I am down on my knees with a heavy tongue of confessions asking that you forgive me. Please look into my life and fix me. I need help that nobody can give me but you. My heart is aching for you now oh father I need you. What am I suppose to do if I don't have you in my life. I feel all alone without you my lord and savior Jesus Christ. I'm ready for a change and to move on too, but I'm not going to move on lord no not without you. So tell me lord what it is that I'm suppose to do. What's my purpose in life, what is it you have for me to do. I want to make you happy and smile at me. So lord show me your way so I can have all the blessings that you have for me.

Strong

Are you really strong because you hold it all in, not showing any signs
of struggle just encouraging others to the end. Keeping
in the inside what others let out, not shedding one tear but watching
them ball out over whatever situation is going on in their life. Speaking
to their pain while yours is locked down. Wondering if they are
listening while all along you supposedly show no doubt.
Listening to them pour out their soul while you hold yours down.
Maintaining this strong hold is it really good for you to do
or should you let down your guard and show them
that you sometime get weak and there isn't
anything unique about you. How could one be strong when
they don't deal with their own pain. Should a person cry alone
and let their tears massage their pain or should
they be with others and share
their pain. So are you really strong by holding it all in or are you as
weak as others but you just hold it all in.

Celebrating The 12th Year of Testaments of the Soul

BONUS

POEMS

Soul Reflections

When I looked into the mirror, I couldn't see myself, what I saw was clearly not me but someone that I felt compelled to help. My empathy grew for this person as I felt her pain, oh my God who is this person, please help her before she goes insane. Her eyes are empty and it seems she has no soul, what happened to this girl? Does anybody know. Why is she in my mirror, blocking my face, it's been a long time since I looked in the mirror and selfishly, I need her to step aside so I can see my face. My patience is running thin and for whatever reason she keeps mimicking what I do, you know what I was going to help this girl but now she is being rude. She looks a mess and so sad too, I hope I am able to help her when she steps out of my way so I can do what I can do.

The Lord Is My Poetry

I am filled with so much joy just thinking about you.
Nothing could compare to the love I have for you.
You have blessed me in so many ways, till I can't even think.
Think of all the many ways you have blessed me, because you don't stop. Looking passed my many flaws & imperfections, correcting me when I am wrong, teaching me a lesson, a lesson that you some way or some how turn into a blessing. Learning how to only focus on what you will think because in the end you are the judge, so hypocrites will you please cast the first stone. My Lord, you have been so good to me, I must exclaim! Our relationship is like no other, there's no doubt. You are the only one that really understands me, & allows me to express it with the gift of poetry, poetry that you have blessed me with, to write creatively. Pure, perfect, ya that's you, & I have fallen deeply in love with you.
You are the one that makes my heart smile, you protect my soul & keep my spirits up, I can't help but testify. Testify about how good you are to me, you always on time, & always there for me.
My Lord you are my poetry.

Conversations....

It's the first time in a long time that we have come face to face. Do you mind, put that drink down & wipe the smile off your face. Why you pretend all the time, you know I know the deal, about how you be tore up inside & can barely feel. You always so good to people, laughing & joking, it's sad they don't know that you really cloaking. Cloaking the hurt you hold inside, with the pain running down your face. So teary eyed, behind the walls, I see the trace on your face. I am reaching out now letting you know that I am here & I understand. I understand that I will motivate, encourage & love you the best way that I can. No more being lonely while surrounded by people or yelling in a quiet, full room of deaf silent people. I am here, you woke me up, I am sorry to say, it just took me looking in the mirror at the reflection of my face. I see me.

Equally Yoked Souls

Words are spreaded like peanut butter all over my mind & so many feelings are bouncing all around my heart that I simply can't define. This really good feeling has taken over me and it's hard to hide the smile of my soul that's imprinted all over me. My everyday walk has me feeling jiggly inside, it's like a feeling of someone tickling me but is very settle all throughout my insides. My heart has found a partner that beats the same beat & a soul that's on the same level, that makes it obvious that nobody but God willed these souls to meet. If I try to stop smiling for a moment, it will not work because God has shined a powerful glory all over these two souls that work. This love is on a powerful high, it doesn't fade, it gets more intense & it feels so good. I love you, my sweet endless love that continues to grow, you answered my heart & it opened to be yours forevermore.

Unknown Prayer Sauce

I have never felt so calm in my life. I open my mouth, believed & it manifested in my life. Describing this feeling is hard to do, but I will do my best to explain it to you. It's aspirin to my headache, ice water on a hot day, ketchup on my fries, turkey wings with some rice, it's the love you show waking me up every day & that still doesn't describe that magnificent thing I felt when I knew my prayers was answered that day. How did I know? It had to be that thing I felt & the minute the words came out my mouth, that's one of the best feelings I ever felt. Where did it come from is a question, I ask every day, because I sure can use that feeling after some of the prayers I have been praying. What was so different than that I can't feel that thing now. I open my mouth up, believed, the feeling doesn't come, and my life keep going by. Lord, please hear me & do what you said you will do. I need your help bringing that feeling back Lord, it brought me closer to you.

When a Mother Prays & Love

Every single year I am going to celebrate you. Mom, you were too great of a gift I never asked for but the Lord saw fit to bless me to be born of you. Endless words of goodness are how I would describe you, not just good words, you backed it up with action day & night all the way through. Mom, your prayers are still being answered, I know this to be true, this family has been blessed in some incredible ways because of you. Faith in the Lord navigated your life and you instilled in this family that there is none other greater than the Lord & Savior Jesus Christ. The love you filled this family with lives on inside of each of us as if we are seeing or hearing through us from you. Such a great blessing to have had a magnificent Mother, who we will always miss and be so thankful for the time we all had with you. I love you momma.

A Blessing from The Lord

I opened the door; you came right through. The sky was dark, it was raining and you didn't want it to mess up your hairdo. You opened an umbrella, I wanted to shelter under there too. You looked at me and said no, I don't know you. I liked your honesty, so we turned and walked away. As we made our 1st step on the walkway the rain stopped & the sun immediately came out to play. We were in a world of our own as we walked down the walkway talking & laughing our heads off that day. We parked by each other, with the same color automobile, we thought that was cool. People walked by saying hello, others smiled & stared but I saw only you. We talked forever on the phone later on that night & we have been talking ever since. Through it all I know that it wasn't a coincidence because it's clear that you were heaven sent. Beautiful, loving, caring, strong, understanding, intelligent, very appreciative, hard-working, giving & just so wonderful all the way through. Yes, the Lord out did himself when he blessed me with you.

Family

Lord, I thank you for my family, extended family and the friends you have placed into my life. I have cried, been full of joy, thrown up my hands and been excited among many other things in this blessed lifetime. You see fit to shine your grace on me every day and you energize me with your love that overflows & keep me protected day after day. You blessed me to be who I am today and to have awesome friends and family whose love is like a million bucks. A million bucks of overflowing pure love that massages my heart every single day and my spirit soaks it all up. I can't help but give you praise for being who you are and letting me know that I am highly favored with the wonderful family/friends in my life.

Milton Keynes UK
Ingram Content Group UK Ltd.
UKHW030849151124
451262UK00001B/301

9 798823 035644